CHAMBER MUSIC

by H. VOXMAN

for

THREE CLARINETS, Vol. II

C O N T E N T S . . .

Rubank®

HAL•LEONARD®
CORPORATION

7777 W. BLUEMOUND RD. P.O. BOX 13819 MILWAUKEE, WI 53213

Minuetto and Trio
from Divertimento III

Bb Clarinets

MOZART

Tempo di minuetto

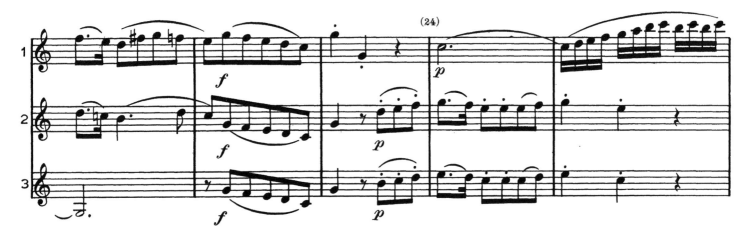

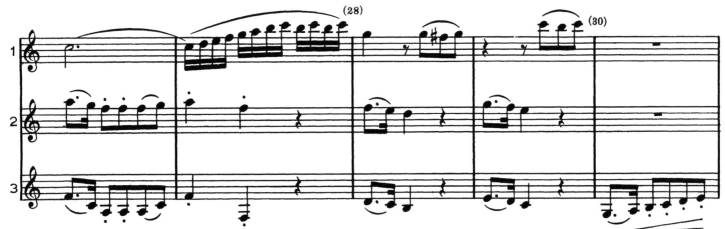

TRIO

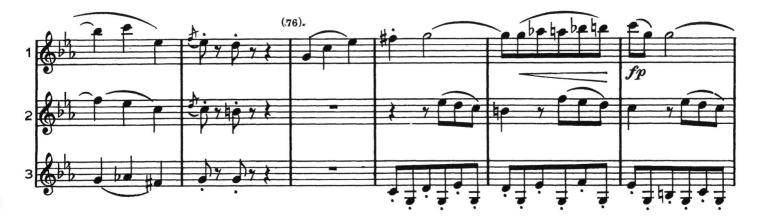

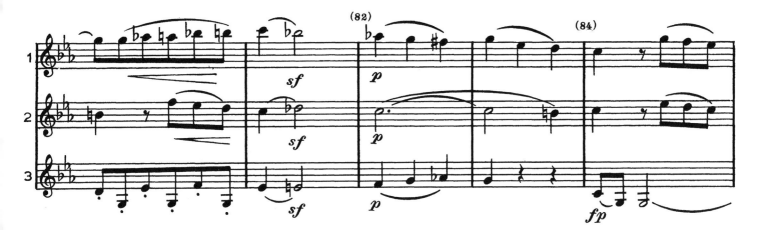

Allegro

B♭ Clarinets

HAYDN

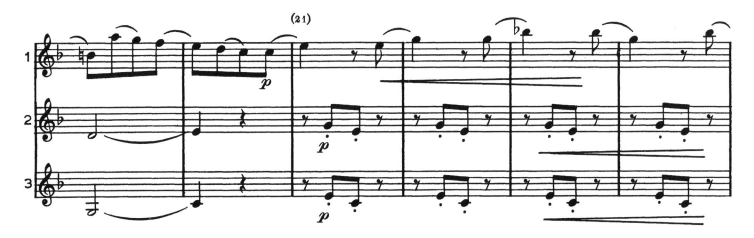

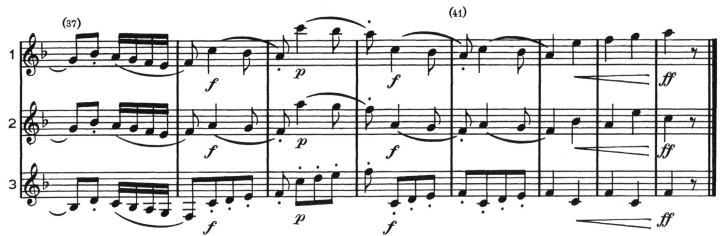

Adagio Sostenuto
from Trio, Op 24

B♭ Clarinets

KUMMER

Adagio sostenuto

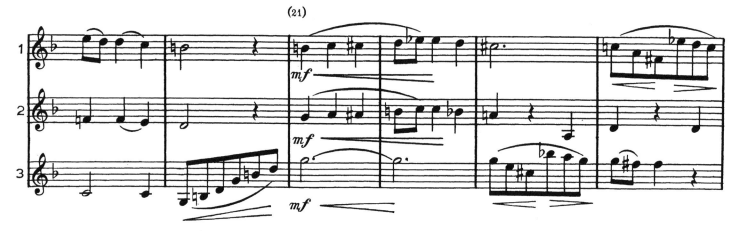

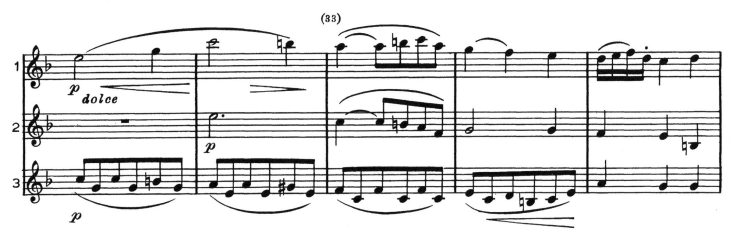

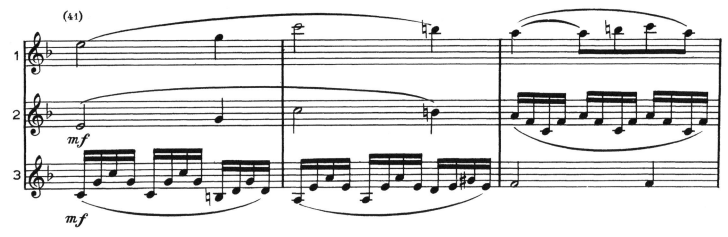

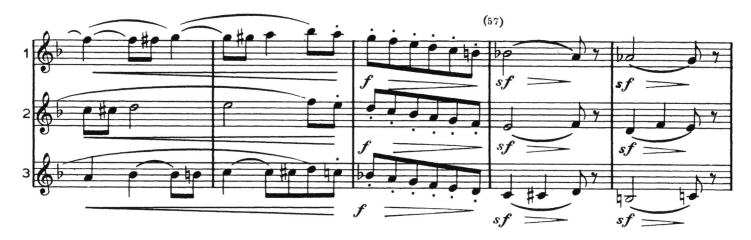

Allegro

from Divertimento IV

B♭ Clarinets

MOZART

Bb Clarinets

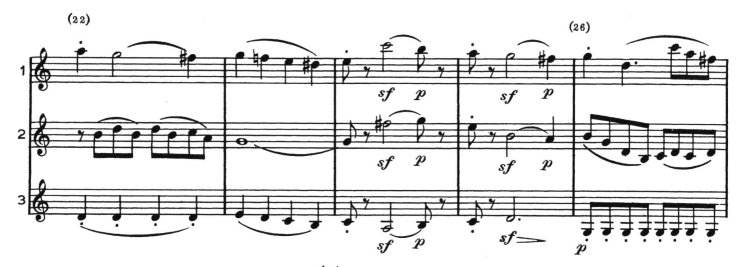

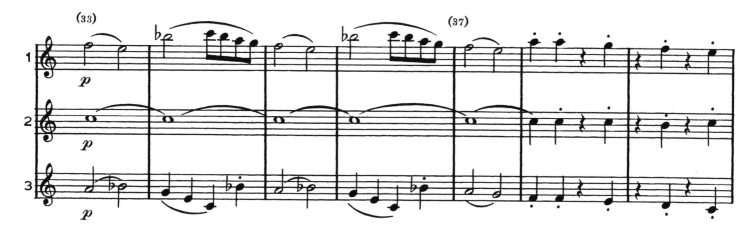

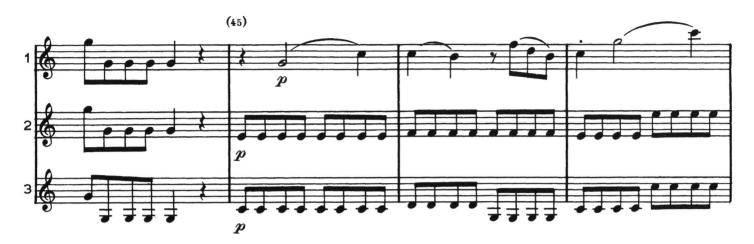

Pastorale

B♭ Clarinets

KRANZ

Andantino

(5)

(9)

(13)

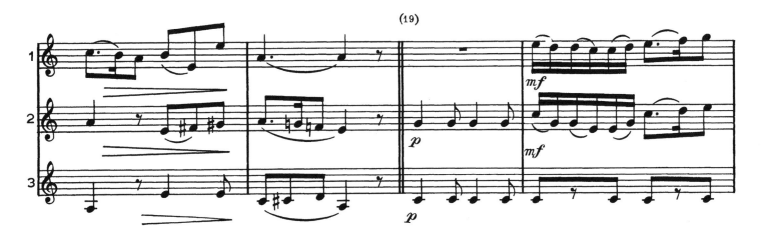

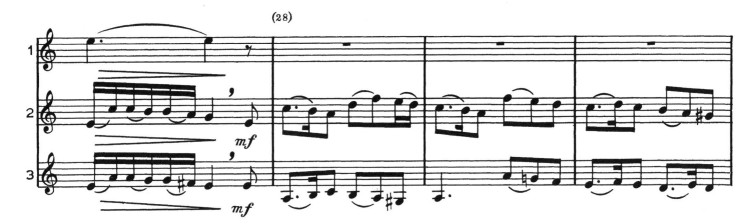

Bb Clarinets

Andante and Allegro

Excerpts from Grand Trio, Op. 8

Bb Clarinets

BOUFFIL

Bb Clarinets

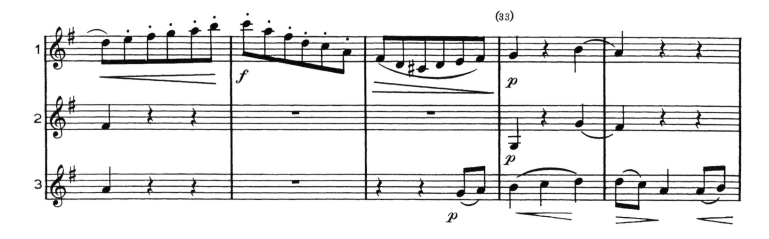

(37)

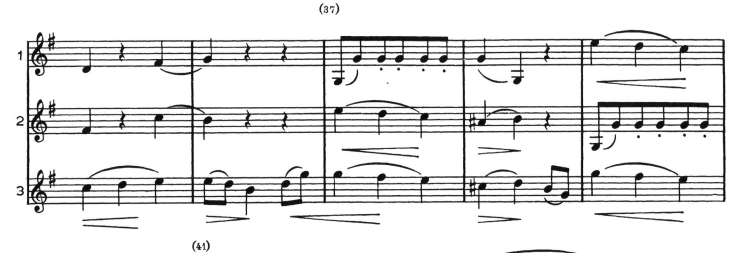

(41)

(45)   (49)

(53)

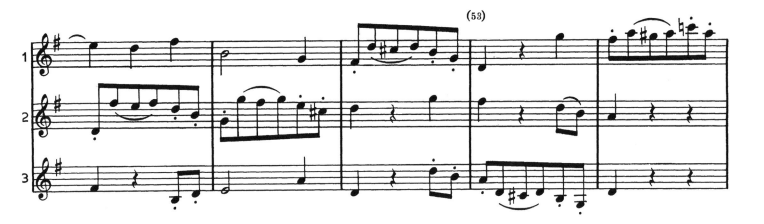

Bb Clarinets

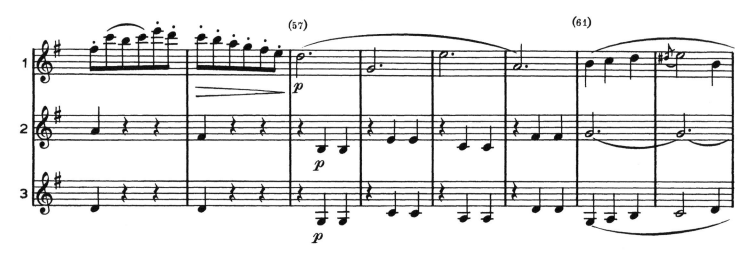

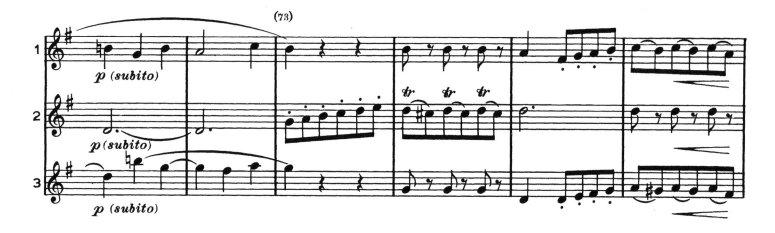

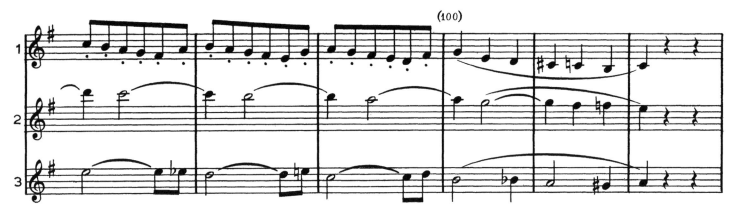

Bb Clarinets

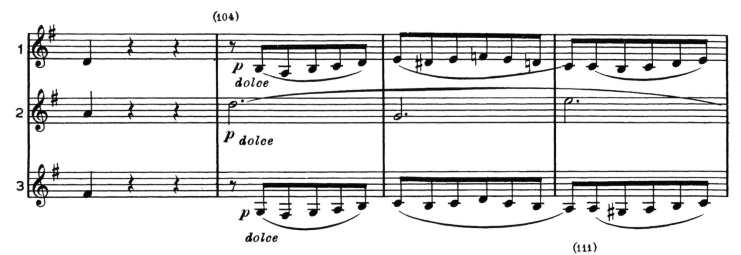

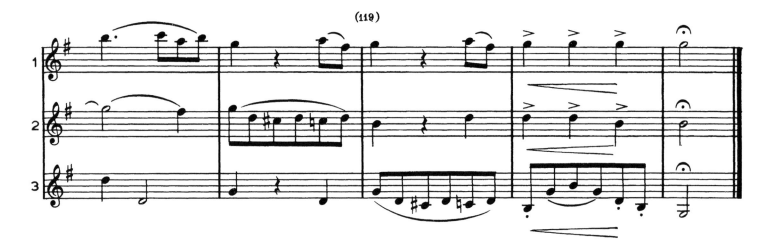

Gavotte en Rondeau

Bb Clarinets

DANDRIEU

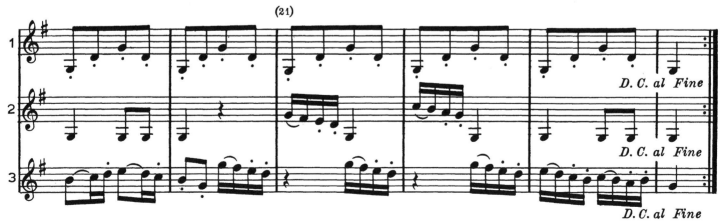

Gavotte

Bb Clarinets

KRANZ

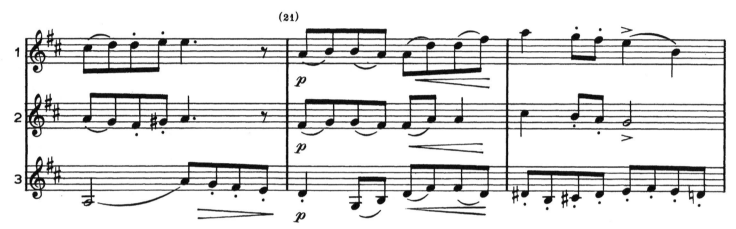

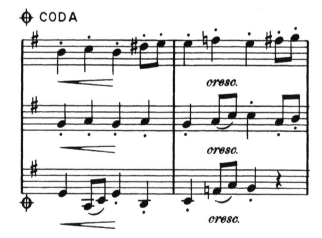

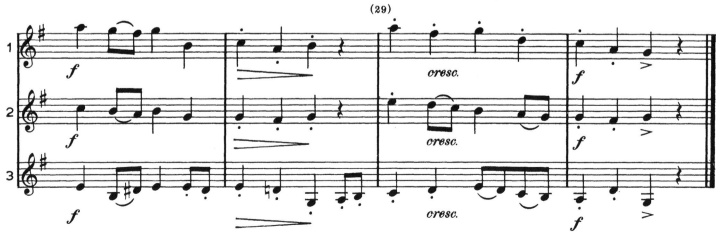

Adagio

from Trio, Op. 87

Bb Clarinets

BEETHOVEN

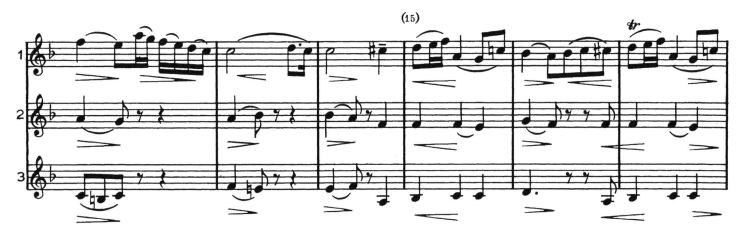

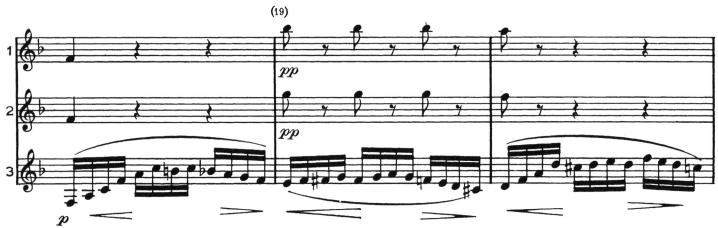

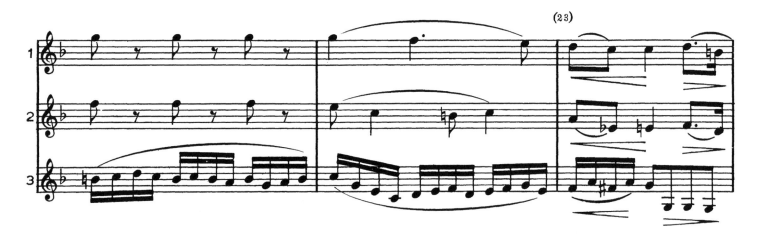

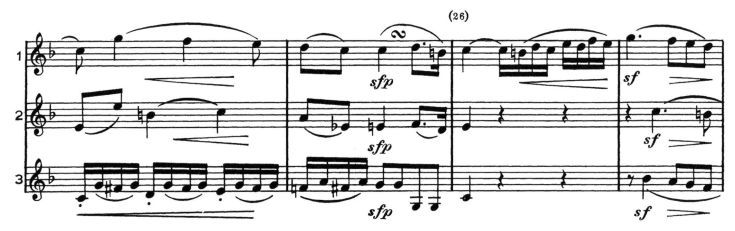

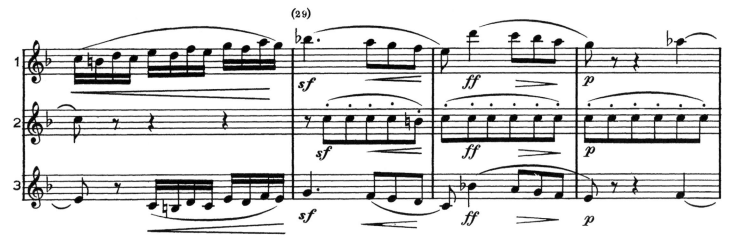

Bb Clarinets

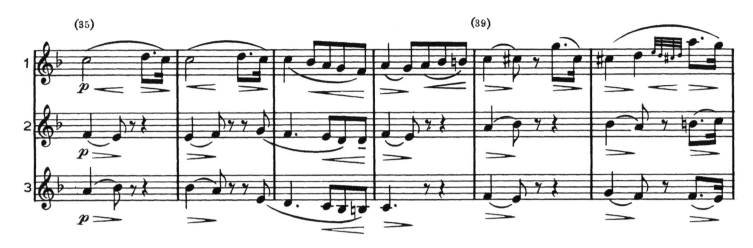

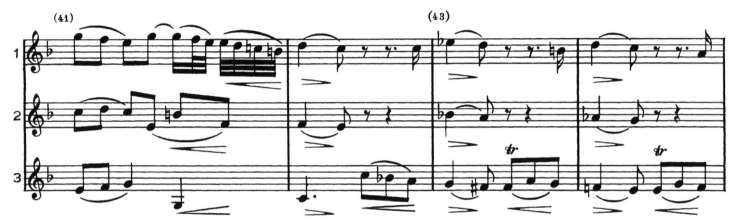

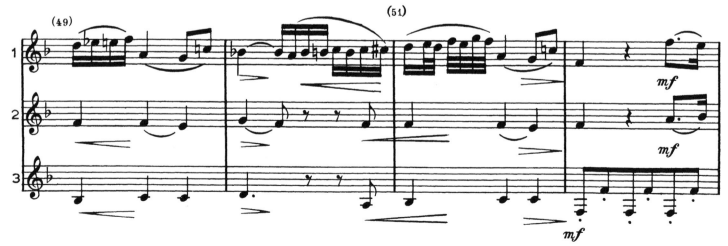

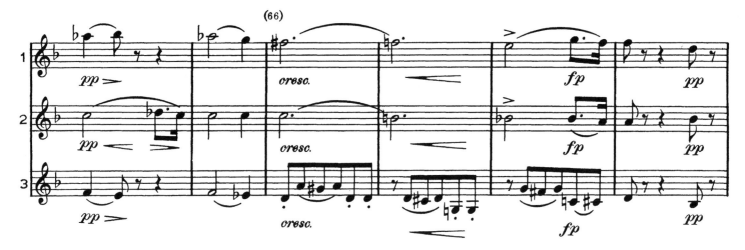

B♭ Clarinets

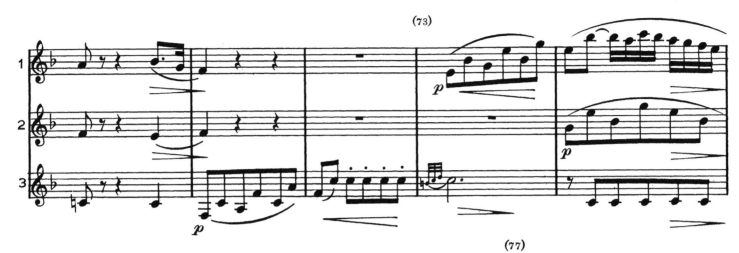

Ländler

KRANZ

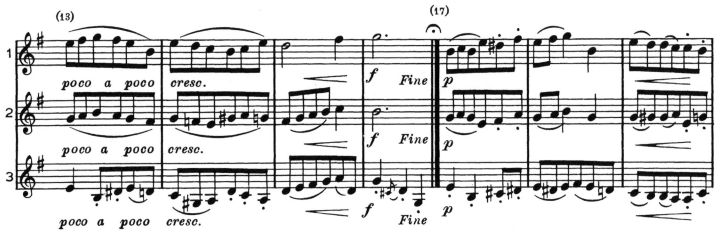

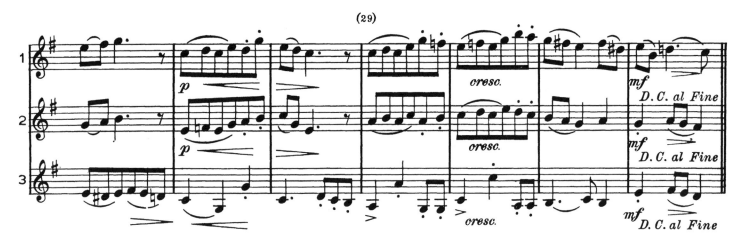

Scherzo

from Grand Trio, Op. 90

Bb Clarinets

KUHLAU

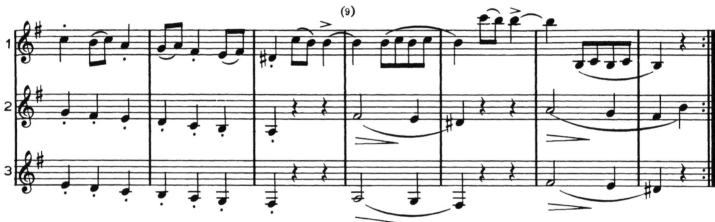

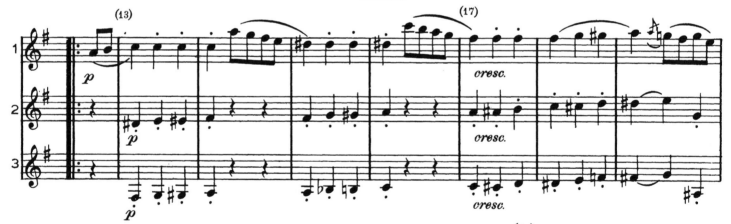

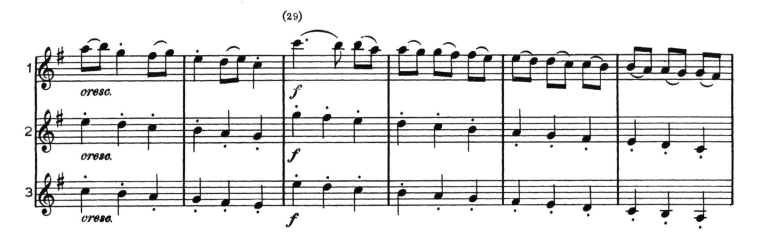

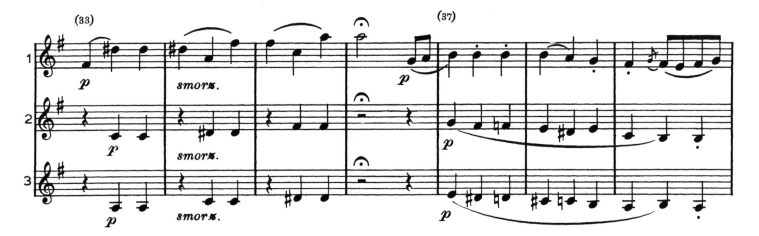

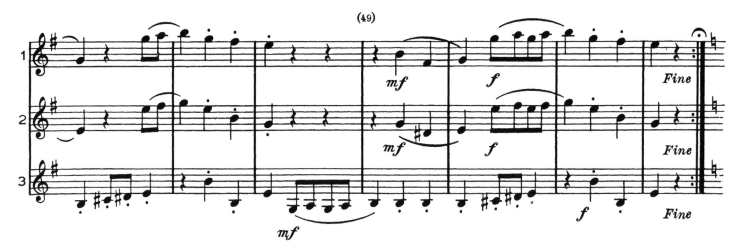

Bb Clarinets

TRIO

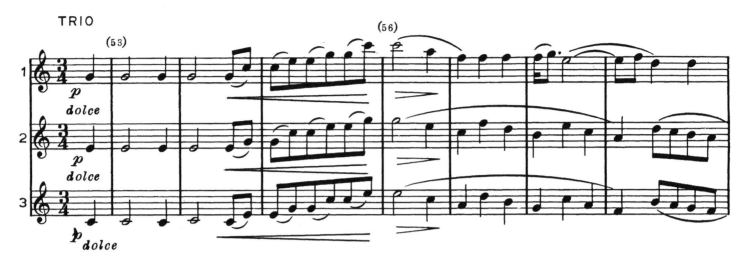

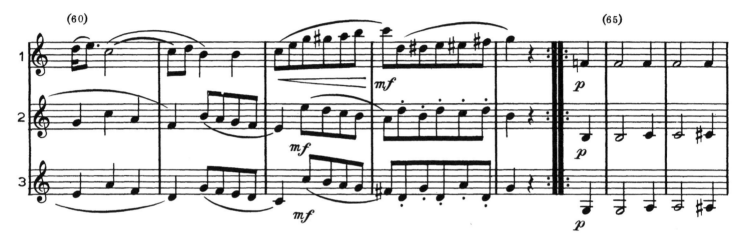

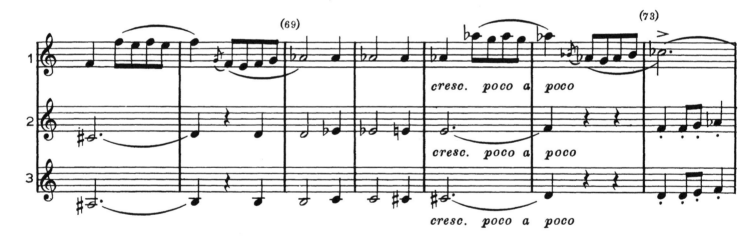

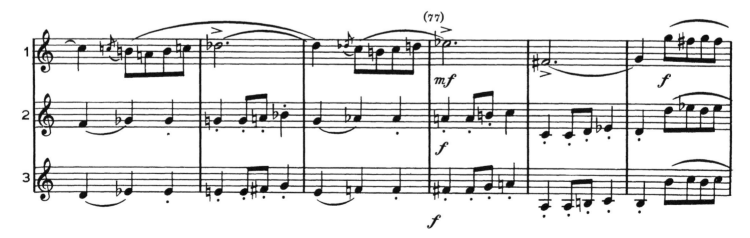

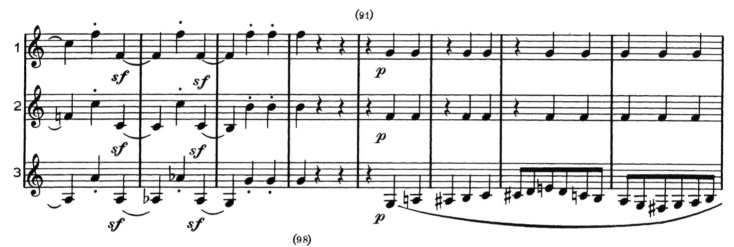

Rondo

from Divertimento IV

B♭ Clarinets

MOZART

Allegretto

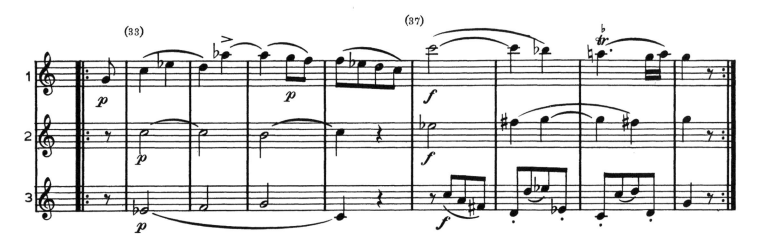

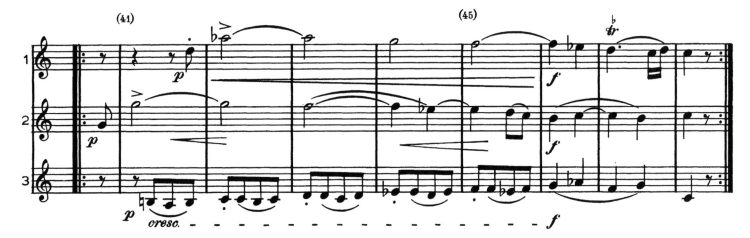

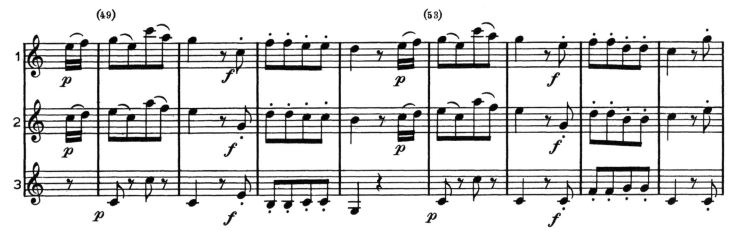

B♭ Clarinets

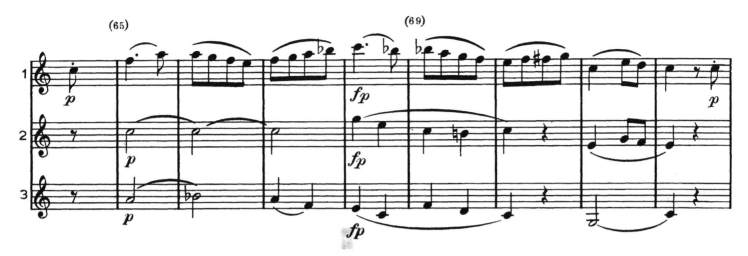

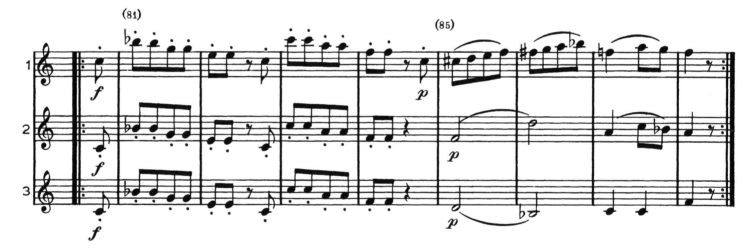

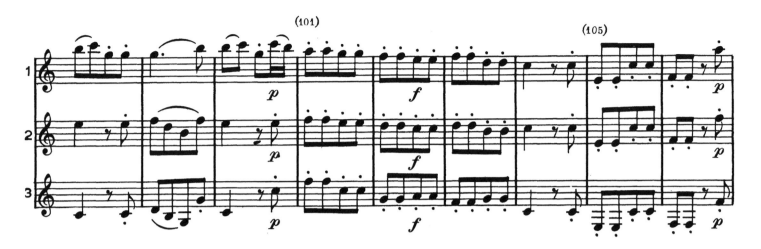

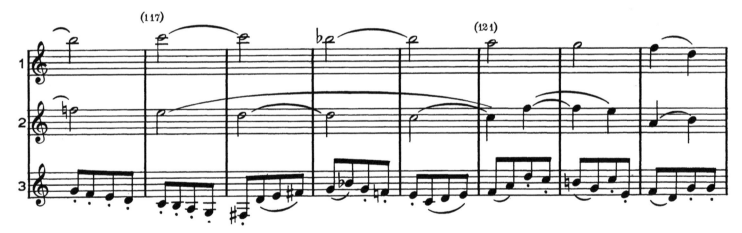

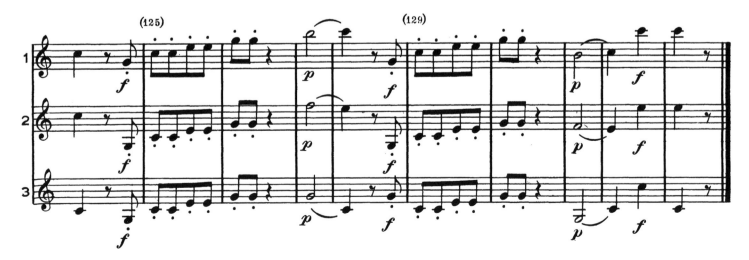

Ha, Ha! This World Doth Pass

Bb Clarinets

WEELKES

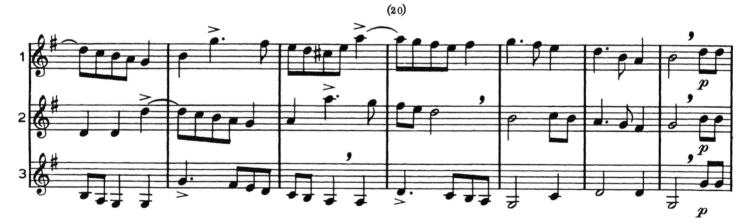